D1527658

What To Do
If You've Missed
The Rapture

What To Do If You've Missed the Rapture
Copyright © 2014 by Joan Lightsey
All rights reserved

Published by
The Lightsey Group
Caring Within Ministries
16112 Foster | Overland Park, KS 66085

ISBN-13: 978-0615960166
ISBN-10: 0615960162

Unless otherwise stated, all Scripture quotations are taken from the King James Version of the Bible.

Printed in the United States of America

What To Do
If You've Missed
The Rapture

by
Joan Lightsey

Table of Contents

Foreword

It is such a privilege to write this foreword for my good friend Joanie, who is an amazing teacher of the Word. In endorsing this book, I am also endorsing a great warrior for the Kingdom of God.

Pastor Joanie is one of those rare individuals who has the courage of her convictions, who will stand for what's right, even when it may be unpopular. I highly respect Joanie's character and God does too!

I think most all people who read the Bible will agree that we're living in the end times. There is going to be a great harvest of souls before the church is taken up so the timing of this book could not be better!

The last part of Ephesians 2:2 (in the Amplified Version) does a magnificent job of describing those who are lost:

> "… the sons of disobedience [the careless, the rebellious, and the unbelieving, who go against the purposes of God]."

First there are "the careless" that have an idea God exists but they are careless and neglectful of their relationship with the Almighty. Then you have "the rebellious" that are offended or believe they must stand against God for whatever reason. And last you have "the unbelieving" who are not aware God is real!

But all are described as going "against the purposes of God." This book is about WAKING THEM UP! Jesus is coming soon and the fields are white unto harvest.

We must get this book into the hands of everyone we can!

Bev Herring
Pastor, Triumphant Life Church
Vice-President, Debt Free Army

Introduction

This book was birthed in my spirit while teaching a series on "Living in the Last Days and End Times Events." That series was developed further and became a three month seminar launched as Bible Prophecy School. This is a Holy Spirit inspired writing to educate, forewarn and instruct people *before* the Rapture happens so they can accept Jesus Christ as savior and not go through the Tribulation.

The end of the Church Age is at hand and Jesus is coming soon!

My desire is to help people understand what has happened at the appearing of Jesus Christ and the catching away of the Church which is called the Rapture. Once all the believers are in Heaven, there is no more restrainer against Satan. Unrestricted sin, immorality, gross darkness and mass deception will become the norm of the day.

This book will help people get through the horrible days of the Tribulation and hopefully find a renewed faith in God.

I truly believe we are living in the last days. Current events in the news confirm many Bible prophecies as we move closer and closer to the Second Coming of Jesus Christ.

Depending on when you're reading this book, the Rapture of the Church may have already happened!

If you are reading this book *before* millions of people have gone missing, there is still time for you to make it right with God by accepting Jesus Christ and securing your eternal salvation.

It is my hope and prayer this book reaches millions of people *before* the Rapture happens and the Tribulation Period begins. But time is running out as we are at the end of the Church Age.

If you are reading this book *after* millions of people have gone missing, the Rapture of the Church has happened. This book will provide *explanations* of what has happened, what will take place in the days ahead and provide suggested *instructions* on what to do going forward.

People need to have a clear understanding of last days end time Bible events, so they won't fall prey to massive deception, which is prevalent now and will only get worse in the days ahead.

I pray you will receive this book by the spirit and not just mere intellect. Let the Holy Spirit minister to your heart as you open your spirit to God's Word. Be Blessed!

Joan Lightsey

Dedication

I want to thank and dedicate this book to my wonderful husband of 26 years, who is also my pastor, Dr. Ernest B. Lightsey for the love, support, prayer and encouragement to help me fulfill God's plan for my life and my dream of being a writer and published author.

Chapter 1

Millions are Missing!

What on earth is happening? People are missing, lots of people! Loved ones have just disappeared! Children are missing and the schools are practically empty. There are so many massive pile-ups on the highways with hundreds dead from car wrecks, the streets look like a war zone! There are dead people on the roads from overturned buses and trains that jumped the tracks. Airplanes are crashing in mid-air and others are just falling from the skies. So many dead, yet so many more are missing! Gone. Vanished. Nowhere to be found! God help us…

Millions are Missing!

There are missing workers, neighbors, babies, toddlers and children, young people, old people, family members and friends. What is going on? People are crying out to God for answers. Have you tried to call your pastor, priest or church leader?

Can you reach them? Probably not, because all the phones lines are jammed. Most, but certainly not all, religious leaders are nowhere to be found. How many times have you emailed or texted your loved ones and have not received a response? Where is your mom, dad or your grandparents? Have you been able to reach them or gone by the house?

What is really going on here? Is there a common thread for all the missing people? Have they been taken captive? Was there an alien invasion or an attack of the zombies? Maybe they are just hiding somewhere. You've gone by the house and no one is home and they are not at work. You have so many questions, yet nobody has any answers. So many people have just vanished into thin air and there is crying and heartbreak and mass chaos everywhere.

So let's stop and think what (if anything) did all the missing people have in common? Is there a common thread? And why are *they* missing and *you* are still here? Well, the one thing all the missing have in common is that they were true Christians, sold-out and living for the Lord. They were all were born-again believers!

What has happened with all certainty is the... *"Rapture of the Church!"*

Jesus Christ, the only begotten son of God Almighty has returned and taken those called by His name home to Heaven. Those Christians who were truly born-again in their hearts, having accepted Jesus as savior and lord in their lives are not missing at all, they are in Heaven. All the innocent little babies and young children up to a certain age (of the age of accountability to make their own decision for Christ) have also been caught up to Heaven.

What has happened is called the "Rapture" or the "catching away" of the Church

The word "rapture" itself is not found in the Bible, but the Christian term "rapture" comes from the Latin word "rapio" that means: to catch up, to snatch away, or to take out. Your friends and family who were born-again believers have been taken out of the earth, caught up and called out by Jesus Christ.

Surely this is very difficult to hear, maybe even harder to believe and understand, but it is true. The Bible has foretold of this event in the Holy Scriptures. The scriptures will confirm what has happened and what will be happening in the days ahead. God is still on the throne! God is still God, Jesus is still the Son of God and the ministry of the Holy Spirit is still on the earth. The world as we knew it, has stepped over into a new phase, a different dimension.

The Church Age is over because "the church" or born-again believers are now in Heaven. The dispensation (time) of grace is now complete and the time of judgment is upon the earth. This book will provide detailed information on what to do, some of which should be done immediately!

Where Shall We Start?

It's always good to start with prayer: "I pray your eyes be opened recognize Jesus Christ is the way, truth and life. I pray you recognize that Jesus is the only way to be reconciled to God. I pray you accept Jesus Christ as your savior and lord, and live a committed Christian life in the time remaining. I pray you share with others these simple Bible truths and get them saved too." Amen.

So Why Am I Still Here?

The reason you are still here and didn't go to Heaven in the Rapture lies solely on what you did with Jesus Christ, whether you accepted or rejected Him. And not making a decision for Christ amounts to making a decision against Christ. Simply believing that God exists is not enough. Lots of people believe or affirm something greater than man exists. The Word says that's not enough, you must be born-again. Others may think they are automatically going to Heaven because of their Christian parents. Sorry, but it doesn't work like that!

Every person must make up their own minds and come to know Jesus for themselves.

Some people presume going to church is good enough and that being a decent, kind or good person is enough to get you to Heaven.

Unfortunately, that is a common misconception and not true. You may even heard some people say they will *"get religion"* when they're older and have had all their fun and are done with sleeping around, ready to quit getting high and drunk and only have a few wild partying days left in them. But tomorrow is not promised to anyone!

Then some people were just too engrossed in watching sports, playing video games or working too hard to even care or even think about God. Yet others got angry at a preacher and offended at the Word being preached, and left the church and also God.

Some only went to church to fulfill their religious obligation, to hear an amazing choir or to meet women, but were not really interested in the gospel message. And last but not least, of course this group of people will also be left behind: the atheists and the agnostics.

These are just a few possible reasons people will be left behind and were not ready for the return of Jesus Christ and the Rapture of the Church.

A lot of people that are left behind will be even more upset with God realizing that the Word of God was indeed true, the Rapture of the Church has happened and they remain here for the days of tribulation and judgment yet to unfold.

I find it ironic that we live in a world of reality shows, singing and dancing competitions, fashion, and cupcake and cooking competitions all to be judged for fame and fortune; people travel to various cities and stand in line for hours to audition all for the chance to be "judged" but nobody wants God or his Holy Word to judge them!

When it comes to real life reality and you try to tell folks they are going the wrong way, doing the wrong things, and headed down a path they have no idea how harsh the consequences will be, they scream "you are so judgmental" or "stop judging me!"

If the Rapture has already happened, the hour of God's wrath and judgment has come. Whatever the reason is that you are still here after the Rapture, just know that you can still make it right with God!

With all the chaos that ensues following the Rapture of the Church, what is now of the utmost importance is to get right with God. Take heart in knowing that you can still accept Jesus, you can still be saved and go to Heaven!

Yes, you can still be saved from what happens next, the wrath and judgment of God upon unrepentant mankind. You can still get born-again by accepting Jesus Christ into your heart. Believe me when you know what's coming in the days ahead, you do not want to be on the earth during the Great Tribulation.

Get Right with God!

The Bible teaches there must be a sacrifice for sin. Man is born with a sin-nature. This came from the fall of Adam back in the Garden of Eden. In the Old Testament, there were animal sacrifices in the holy temple of God, whereby the blood of goats and sheep were poured on the Alter to atone for man's sins. This only covered sin. God provided for the remission of sin and reconciliation to Himself through the ultimate and final sacrifice for sin through His Son Jesus Christ. He suffered the passion of the cross at Calvary for our sins so that we can be reconciled back to God.

We are all in need of a savior and the one true savior is Jesus Christ. Receiving Jesus Christ as savior and lord is the one and only true pathway to be reconciled to God. Salvation is a free gift from God, one we do not deserve nor could we ever earn. To be saved or born-again means your "spirit-man" which is the real you, has a change of nature.

This is more than just a change of heart. It is born-again from spiritual death (because sin separates man from God) and is born-again from death to life, everlasting life through Jesus Christ. This means spending eternity with Jesus and not eternally separated from God. These scriptures help explain salvation further:

John 5:24

> He that heareth my word, and believeth on him that sent me, hath everlasting life, and shall not come into condemnation; but is passed from death unto life.

Romans 10:9-10

> That if thou shalt confess with thy mouth the Lord Jesus, and shalt believe in thine heart that God hath raised him from the dead, thou shalt be saved. For with the heart man believeth unto righteousness; and with the mouth confession is made unto salvation.

Let's take time right now, don't waste another minute before making things right with God. Let's pray:

"Dear Jesus, I believe you are the son of God, born of a virgin, crucified, buried and raised from the dead, sitting now in Heaven at the right hand of God. I repent and turn away from sin and unbelief. Forgive me of my sins. Thank You for laying down your life for me on the cross at Calvary. I invite you to come into my heart and receive you now as my Savior and Lord. I am now saved, born-again. From this day forward I'm going to live for You, Amen!"

Praise the Lord! If you truly meant that prayer in your heart and have accepted Jesus Christ as savior and lord, you are now saved! Your spirit is now born-again with new life in Jesus Christ. You will now spend eternity *with* God and not separated *from* God!

What "Being Saved" Means

Man is a spirit being, who has a soul (which is the mind, will and emotions) and lives in a physical body. It is the inside man, the real you, the spirit of man that is born again and made brand new. The old sin nature is gone and new nature seeks God and desires the things of God. Romans 12:1-2 instructs born-again believers to live holy (not according to the old sin nature) and to be transformed by the renewing of the mind. This means to learn about God, His ways of living, doing things and being right. We are all spirit beings that live eternally forever in one place (Heaven with God) or in the other place (Hell with Satan). For the sake of time, this book will not debate the existence of Heaven and Hell. God's word tells us they both exist. Heaven and Hell are real. Both are real physical places. Heaven is a planet that exists outside of the realm that man can see with vast telescopes.

Hell is a literal place in the center of the earth, a place of torment, sorrow and loneliness, a place of pain and agony, a place of endless suffering from burning fire.

21

It was made for Satan and his cohorts (fallen angels) and for **not** for man; but it was created for those who hate God, rebel against God and just flat out refuse to accept Jesus. Hell is a place of eternal judgment forever separated from God.

Now That You Are Born-Again

If the Rapture has already happened and you are just now getting born-again, know that you can still be translated or caught up to Heaven midway through the Tribulation and miss the wrath of the Great Tribulation. Now that's good news! It's vitally important to understand salvation and eternity so that you are able to share the gospel message with family, friends and other loved ones.

Sharing Jesus Christ and the love of God with others is called the "good news" of the gospel of Jesus Christ. After the Rapture, it will be really good news because people will need to know they can still be saved and accept Jesus Christ! All is not lost!

"Propaganda and Deception will be widespread and mainstream"

With millions missing and those remaining probably losing their minds in the midst of all the turmoil, it will be imperative that you share the peace and salvation found only in Jesus Christ with others. People will need answers, not just any old answers, they will need the truth!

Those left behind will need to know about the comfort of the Holy Spirit. They need to understand the truth about what has transpired and where their missing loved really are, so they won't be deceived. They will believe the lies being perpetrated through various sources unless someone like you shares the truth about God, the Rapture and Heaven, or at the very least share this book with them!

After the Rapture, false preaching and teaching will be on the rise. Spreading falsehoods about Jesus and the Rapture will be rampant and false religions will grow at a phenomenal pace deceiving many.

But the truth remains that Jesus Christ is the only way to receive forgiveness of sins and to be reconciled to Almighty God.

The messages in this book are not popular even today *before* the Rapture of the Church. The gospel of Jesus Christ is rapidly becoming more and more offensive to the world. We even live in a day and age where talking about God and openly sharing Jesus is increasingly being viewed as hate speech. With this shift in our post modern culture, talking about Jesus Christ will most assuredly become a hate crime after the Rapture; but the fact remains true that man must be born-again and the gospel must still be shared!

I hope you are reading this book *before* the Rapture of the Church and will take steps necessary to make sure your eternal salvation is secure in Christ; and after that, you must get busy about sharing this message with your family and friends. There's no time to be apprehensive or concerned about whether you will be received or liked, you must move past that fear and tell them the truth.

Believe me… you do not want your loved ones to go through the Tribulation Period!

Chapter 2

The Rapture of the Church
(Explanations)

The Rapture, or the catching away or the snatching out of the Church is prophesied in the Holy Scriptures. But what is the Rapture really?

The Rapture is an event where one day very soon Jesus Christ will appear in the skies and will call up (snatch out or carry away) the Church, which are true born-again Christians and supernaturally move them to Heaven. The Rapture is explained as one of many key events in Bible prophecy that precede the Second Coming of Christ. This is not the end of the world because the world never ends; it just changes from one age and time (dispensation) to a new age and time which is called the Millennial Reign of Jesus.

What follows next in time is a seven (7) year period in which the Bible calls "a time of great tribulation upon the earth."

Believe the Bible when it says the Tribulation Period will be a time of great suffering and distress with God's wrath (judgment) being poured out on the earth. God has not appointed His children unto wrath, and all the Church (born-again believers) will be removed from the earth *before* God's final judgment begins. Some teach Christians will go through the Tribulation Period, but that does not align with the Holy Scriptures:

> Romans 5:9 Much more then, being now justified by his blood, we shall be saved from wrath through him.
>
> 1 Thessalonians 1:10 And to wait for his Son from Heaven, whom he raised from the dead, even Jesus, which delivered us from the wrath to come.
>
> 1 Thessalonians 5:9 For God hath not appointed us to wrath, but to obtain salvation by our Lord Jesus Christ.

Additional References: Isaiah 13:8-10, Jeremiah 10:10

The Tribulation is the time set aside for Israel to come to know and acknowledge Jesus as the Messiah (the Sent One) and to reconcile the Jewish people back to God as prophesied in Daniel 9:27. The Tribulation Period is not a time designated for Christians. The church had over 2,000 years to receive Jesus Christ. The "Church Age" was concluded with the catching away of the Christians from the earth and moving them to Heaven.

So How Did the Rapture Happen?

At the fulfillment of time, which is only known to God (not even Jesus knows), God turned to Jesus Christ and said something like "the fullness of time has come, it is time, go get my children!"

And in that same moment, Jesus Christ stepped out of Heaven and onto the clouds accompanied by angels, appearing (or will yet appear) in the skies and with the sound of a Heavenly trumpet and the shout of an archangel one of the greatest miracles of the Bible takes place when Jesus said "come up hither" (Revelation 4:1). No one knows the day or the hour when Jesus will come back, but we must be ready and looking for His return.

I Thessalonians 5:2 (NASB)

> For you yourselves know full well that the day of the Lord will come just like a thief in the night.

All born-again believers living for the Lord at the time of the Rapture, those called by His name were taken out of the earth and went up to Heaven with Jesus! The Bible says this happened quickly, at the twinkling of an eye all were "changed" from mortal to immortal. There was no death, no pain, but only joy for the Christians being translated to Heaven!

Ever wonder about First Thessalonians 4:16 which states: *the dead in Christ will rise first?*

I Thessalonians 4:13-17 (NASB)

But we do not want you to be uninformed, brethren, about those who are asleep, so that you will not grieve as do the rest who have no hope. [14] For if we believe that Jesus died and rose again, even so God will bring with Him those who have fallen asleep in Jesus. [15] For this we say to you by the word of the Lord, that we, who are alive and remain until the coming of the Lord, will not precede those who have fallen asleep. [16] For the Lord Himself will descend from Heaven with a shout, with the voice of *the* archangel and with the trumpet of God, and the dead in Christ will rise first. [17] Then we who are alive and remain will be caught up together with them in the clouds to meet the Lord in the air, and so we shall always be with the Lord.

And if that wasn't super awesome enough for you, let's look at additional scriptures explaining that marvelous awe-inspiring miracle of the catching away or Rapture of the church:

1 Corinthians 15:51-54

[51]Behold, I shew you a mystery; We shall not all sleep, but we shall all be changed, [52] In a moment, in the twinkling of an eye, at the last trump: for the trumpet shall sound, and the dead shall be raised incorruptible, and we shall be changed. [53]For this corruptible must put on incorruption, and this mortal must put on immortality. [54]So when this corruptible shall have put on incorruption, and this mortal shall have put on immortality, then shall be brought to pass the saying that is written, Death is swallowed up in victory.

The great miracle of the resurrection of the bodies of the dead in Christ (born again believers who have already died), will be resurrected to meet Jesus Christ in the air. What a glorious day it will be when the saints in Heaven are reconnected with their new glorified bodies (flesh and bone, no blood).

Just think about all the bodies that have been cremated, badly burned or dismembered will come back together and meet Him in the skies! You may be thinking, what about those who were lost at sea, or whose physical bodies were not found or were mutilated? Good question, glad you asked!

After the Resurrection, Jesus Christ was given <u>all power</u> in Heaven and in earth, that very same creative power of God that made the Heavens and the earth. He will speak to the seas to give up the dead, and from ashes to ashes and from dust to dust, bodies will be miraculously resurrected and recreated (if need be) to be reconnected with their spirit being in Heaven.

Why do people already in Heaven need a recreated immortal body?

The saints of God will live forever on the new earth. Christians will not become angels floating on clouds for eternity, but will come back to earth with Jesus Christ exactly 7-years after the Rapture, to rule and reign with Him.

The immortal saints (the church in heaven) rule, reign and govern the saints who were in Heaven for thousands of years and the people on the earth that made it through the Great Tribulation (most will be born-again and but not all).

Jesus Christ and the Heavenly host defeat Satan in the Battle of Armageddon, which takes place in the valley of Megiddo at the end of the 7-year Tribulation Period. Under the influence of Satan, the 200 million man army is utterly defeated and destroyed.

When Jesus comes back to earth, this is called the Second Advent or the Second Coming of Jesus Christ (and is not to be confused with the Rapture).

At the Second Coming, Jesus Christ comes back to earth clothed in an illustrious white garment and is riding a beautiful white horse. All the Heavenly host returns with Him. He comes to defeat Satan and then will setup His earthly kingdom in Jerusalem.

He reigns and rules during the 1,000 year period and all the saints in Heaven come back to earth with Him. This is why those in Heaven will need their bodies... we all come back to live on the new earth!

It is good to know that when Satan is defeated, bound and thrown into the pit of Hell and is sealed up for 1,000 years, there will be no temptation, no sin, no sickness, no disease and no death on the earth. Glory to God!

A new time and dispensation begins which is called the Millennial Reign. Jesus reigns from the Temple in Jerusalem and this fact alone should shed some light on why there is such a fight in the Middle East for the control of the city of Jerusalem! Satan probably thinks that having control of the city of Jerusalem may prevent, hinder or impede the return of Jesus, but thank God it won't!

How Did The Rapture Happen?

In the supernatural catching away or the Rapture of the church, Jesus did not physically come back and step down on the earth. Jesus Christ and the angels appeared in the clouds as prophesied in Revelation 4:1 which says:

> "After this I looked, and, behold, a door was opened in Heaven: and the first voice which I heard was as it were of a trumpet talking with me; which said, Come up hither, and I will shew thee things which must be hereafter."

It is hard to even imagine how it will feel to never taste death! For those who are caught away in the Rapture, the physical body was (or will be) instantly changed from a mortal human body to immortality, which is a glorified body that lives forever and ever and ever. Glory to God! We will be just like Jesus after the resurrection, living eternally in an immortal body which has flesh and bone (but no blood).

Luke 24:38-39 (NIV)

> He said to them, "Why are you troubled, and why do doubts rise in your minds? Look at my hands and my feet. It is I myself! Touch me and see; a ghost does not have flesh and bones, as you see I have."

The scriptures reveal that we will be just like Jesus. After he was raised from the dead, he remained on the earth for many days. He was seen by many people and had several meetings and even had dinner with the disciples before his ascension back to Heaven. Yes we will recognize and know one another just as disciples knew Jesus, we'll eat and fellowship just as Jesus did. We can be translated from one place to another very quickly because we will have glorified bodies, just like Jesus, with no fleshly limitations.

One difference between Jesus Christ coming at the time of the Rapture versus the Second Coming: Jesus does not physically come down to earth.

He calls the Church to "come up hither" and supernaturally all the born-again believers meet Him in the skies and are taken up into Heaven for 7 years.

The last discussion of the church is in Revelation Chapter 4. Not much else is mentioned about the church until Revelation Chapter 19 when it describes all of the preparation for the Marriage Supper of the Lamb.

Subsequent chapters describe what's going on in Heaven and other chapters detail the horrific judgments taking place on the earth during the Tribulation Period.

Final Thoughts

If you are reading this book *__after__* the Rapture event has happened, take heart in knowing your loved ones are not lost or missing, they haven't been zapped or kidnapped by aliens; they were not vaporized, nor were they annihilated by some unexplainable cosmic mishap or cataclysmic event.

> John 13:1-4 I will receive you unto Myself, that where I am, there you may be also.

> Ephesians 1:10 "… that in the dispensation of the fullness of the times He might gather together in one all things in Christ, both which are in Heaven and which are on earth in Him."

I hope you can find comfort in knowing your loved ones have seen Jesus Christ face to face! They are worshipping God in the throne room of Heaven. They are the only group of people there (with the exception of two Old Testament witnesses) who have never tasted death. How glorious is that! Not even Jesus can claim that, for Jesus died and rose from the grave. Imagine your children, mom, dad, grandma and other family members in Heaven right now praising God alongside the disciples Matthew, Mark, Luke and John!

They have talked with Mary the Mother of Jesus and are now walking on heavenly streets of gold with Noah, Moses and Abraham! Everyone is on their way to that great Heavenly banquet called the Marriage Supper of the Lamb.

What a wonderful time that will be. Jesus said he would come back for those that belong to Him and He did. Will you be ready?

Chapter 3

What Happens Now?
(Explanations and Instructions)

After the Rapture and during the Tribulation Period, as a Christian your life could possibly be in danger. Yes danger! This will be a horrific time filled with dreadful days, mass deception will be covering the earth and people will not know who to trust.

Sure some churches will still be open, but most of them will be the post-modern secular progressive (apostate) churches that do not honor or adhere to the Holy Scriptures. New believers in Jesus Christ will eventually be forced to worship the Lord "underground" as society continues to grow increasingly hostile and overwhelmingly anti-God. Every day Christians will become more outcast, criticized and viewed as haters of good. The Bible says the days will come when evil is revered as good, and good is seen as evil. We are now living in those days!

With Millions of People Gone...

What will happen in the workplace? Will the people left behind still have to go to work? What about all those who are now gone, what happens to their bank accounts, investments, their homes? What happens in the U.S. and global economies around the world?

All around the world millions of people will simply be gone from workforce. Just think about it... do you really think those remaining will be going to work the next day or week? Probably not! Most people will be so distraught over their missing children and family members, it will be days, maybe even weeks before people are able to even think straight, let alone go back to work. There will be considerable job abandonment. When some folks are able to return to work, they will be apprehensive about their paychecks clearing what remains of the collapsed banking system. In just one single event, the already crumbling U.S. monetary system and money markets will fail and the markets will crash.

"This will cause mass hysteria and a run on the banks"

Across the world, economies will fall like dominos. Rioting and looting will be at the forefront as people will be stricken with fear and overwhelming grief and sorrow. People will be afraid to venture outside of their homes.

It will be only a matter of days before there begins to be substantial food shortages due to lack of production and non-delivery. Medical and prescription drug supplies will begin to dwindle, pharmacies will have to close and many more unfathomable situations and circumstances will unfold as the world tries to figure out how to regroup from the "disappearances" or the "so called Rapture" event.

Martial Law and Money From Friends

The government will invoke martial law to curb the panic and violence as they try to figure out how to manage this nationwide crisis. There will be military enforced mandatory curfews instituted to curb the rioting, crime and violence and maintain some semblance of order.

Since the U.S. economy has not yet fully recovered from the 2008 recession, the government will struggle to meet entitlement payments as the tax base lost millions of payers into the system. Monthly checks could be limited or decreased in amount or could even be temporarily halted. As a result, inflation will skyrocket while the government tries to figure out what to do. Some semblance of stability in the markets will be restored as our solvent nation friends (like Russia, China, Saudi Arabia or the UAE) will step up to loan the U.S. more money to survive in the short term and the debt ceiling will be entirely removed. But are these nations, in which we are already heavily indebted to, really our friend?

And if the economic instability isn't bad enough, also consider that this be a most opportune time for the terrorists living in America and other home grown radicals to perpetrate a strike against the U.S.? God have mercy. The future will be filled with terribly dreadful days as the vestiges of life, liberty and the pursuit of happiness take a backseat to the new norm of survival of the fittest.

Those left behind will blame God and the Christians for this world-wide crisis, thus alienating more people from seeking Jesus. The new post-church society will point the finger at Christians for causing all the trouble and further deem Christianity as divisive and harmful, hateful, racist and intolerant and therefore should have no place in post modern society. They will even blame God for all the heartache and hopelessness caused by the disappearances and curse Him for their pain and suffering.

Christianity: An Organized Hate Group

If Christians are being labeled as "haters" now (even before the Rapture), imagine how difficult it will be for the new Christians after the Rapture. During this time (if not sooner) the tax exempt status [501(c)3] afforded to churches and other non-profit religious organizations will be abolished. The church will be defined as a hate group. The government will not allow for tax exempt status to be granted for what will soon be regarded as an organized hate group, which is pretty much what the remaining Church will be called... a bunch of intolerant haters.

"This is forming even now with the war on Christianity"

The world will be looking to the United Nations, not the United States for a leader to calm the storm and bring about peace in this world-wide crisis.

With all this going on the Anti-Christ steps onto the international scene as a new world leader! This new world leader will come as a man of peace, to lead the way out of turmoil (through false hope).

PERFECT TIMING FOR THE RISE OF THE ANTI-CHRIST

With world-wide civil unrest and upheaval, this is the perfect time to introduce the new world order leader. This man will restore civility and order and bring about peace. This man will be a beloved, charismatic leader and even revered as a savior. This man is the *Anti-Christ* who will very quickly rise to power as a world leader, who will take and be given great authority to fulfill Satan's end time agenda.

This newly appointed world leader may head up the 17 member European Union (EU) states and possibly be the new Secretary General of the United Nations.

He may also seize the opportunity to move the UN headquarters from New York to one of the EU nations, possibly the UK (London), Italy or France.

This New World Order leader is the Anti-Christ (Satan's Messenger, the Man of Sin)

Where all other attempts have failed, he will rise to power on a roadmap of peace and will successfully broker a peace treaty with Israel for seven years. Yes, there will finally be peace, albeit a false sense of security kind of peace, in the Middle East!

You should know that Satan cannot create anything! He can only twist and pervert what God has already created. Satan has setup up his demonic kingdom to mimic what God created. Ephesians 6:12 reveals that Satan's kingdom has hierarchal levels (like God's Heavenly host) with principalities, powers, and rulers and even has mocked the trinity with his own:

The Holy Trinity
God, Jesus Christ, and the Holy Spirit

The Satanic Trinity
Satan, Anti-Christ, and the False Prophet

The Anti-Christ will also institute a new (false) religion setup to worship him as "God" and anoints his own religious leader whom the Bible calls the False

Prophet. This new "one world one religion" will most likely come through what will be formerly known as the Roman Catholic Church. It combines the tenets of faith from many religions including Christianity, Islam and Catholicism and its goal is to combine our various Bibles and holy books into a new collaborative holy book. Its beginnings are founded in the goals to recognize we all worship the same God, to advocate "co-existence" as one family under God and by the harmony of the Bible and Quran into a new collective work which could be called something like *Chrislam*.

Do not be deceived by these seemingly honest efforts to bring harmony of the religions and unity to believers. But the core of its foundation is to remove the one true Almighty God.

Let's get back to the Anti-Christ. With the seven year peace treaty with Israel established, the Jewish people operate under a false sense of hope and freedom. The Anti-Christ allows them to rebuild the Temple right next to the Islamic holy site in Jerusalem, known as the Dome of the Rock. The Anti-Christ will be hailed as a great man of peace and will most certainly be given the Nobel Peace Prize. He will be greatly revered, highly esteemed and honored as many fall prey to his deception. It is for this very reason that I have written this book, so you will know what's going to happen in the days ahead.

THE LIST

Do These Things Right Away:

- Get cash - keep cash on hand at all times
- Get and secure a Bible, several if possible
- Stock up on non-perishable food/meats
- Stock up on bottled or gallon jugs of water
- Secure items of self defense, ammo, etc.
- Get many Bible based books, CDs & DVDs
- Keep on hand a weather radio, DVD/CD player
- Purchase a generator, get batteries or a charger
- Purchase lighters (fireplace) or matches in bulk
- Get an old fashioned hand saw, ax or hammer
- First Aid Safety Kit and other medicines
- Find Christians (you can trust) for fellowship

This is a list of instructions and things to do to remain safe and spiritually strong. These are a few items needed for basic safety and survival during the Tribulation. It is not an all-inclusive list, but one to help you get started. We'll discuss "The List" in detail in the next chapters.

Hopefully by now you have accepted Jesus as savior. This is very important because going through the Tribulation, newly born-again believers should not be deceived like the masses of people that will love and follow the Anti-Christ and his False Prophet! The Word of God must be at the forefront of your life.

Those who become born-again Christians after the Rapture need to know and understand that they will only face difficult times for the first 3½ years and then they will also be translated to Heaven. Yes really!

ANOTHER RAPTURE?

In Revelation, Chapter 7 we read about the 144,000 Jewish (unmarried virgin) men who are sealed with the mark of God. They will be evangelists going to and fro on the earth, preaching the gospel of salvation through Jesus Christ the Messiah to the Jewish people (and everyone else too) and thousands upon thousands will come to Christ!

This is the Heavenly assignment of the 144,000 during the first 3½ years. There will be multitudes of Jewish people saved around the world, accepting Jesus Christ as The Sent One. Yes, our Jewish brothers and sisters will get born-again! But sadly, many still will not believe. And yes, other folk (Gentiles) will have the chance to be saved during this time as well.

All those who are born-again at this time will be caught up to Heaven (in a rapture event) along with the 144,000 Jewish evangelists. If you are born-again at this time, you will go Heaven. In Revelation Chapter 7 this group is referred to as "Tribulation Saints" having endured the tough times on earth during the first 3½ years of the Tribulation.

This supernatural catching away happens right at the halfway mark exactly 3½ years, which is 42-months or 1,260 days from the day of the Rapture of the Church. God is precise and always on time!

The next several chapters will discuss items from "The List." Remember these are only suggestions (which are highly recommended) and are not required or mandatory items. But please do take "The List" seriously!

Pray over it and ask the Lord to give you a plan of survival. Only God knows and time will tell what will happen and how difficult it will be during those times. Remember, the God is your source and the Holy Spirit is your helper! Call on the Lord for help and ask for wisdom (James 1: 5-7) in every situation so you won't fall prey to the mass deception and cover ups.

"Deception wouldn't be so deceiving if it wasn't deceptive!"

Chapter 4

The List - Food
(Instructions)

After the Rapture, people will still be living what will become their new normal daily life. No one knows how much daily life will change, but in most instances there will eventually be school and work, shopping, playing sports, hanging out and living as much of a regular life as is humanly possible.

Food

- Stock up on non-perishable food items
- Canned goods like veggies, fruits, meats
- Dried fruits and meats; freeze-dried packets
- Staples like peanut butter/jelly, pancake mix
- Bottled or gallon jugs of water, fruit juices, etc.

Buy all the non-perishable food items you can! As soon as the Rapture occurs, stock up and replenish your pantries!

Purchase items that don't need to be cooked or that can be cooked with only water. Things like rice, pasta, beans, canned vegetables, stuffing, oatmeal and grits, pancake mix and syrup, dried fruit. Stock up on cans of fruit, juices, powdered milk, cocoa mix, etc.

Non-perishable or Freeze-dried food packets
have up to 10-Yr Freshness Guarantee and Shelf Life

Sure you can buy a freezer and fill it with meat and vegetables, but the non-perishable items will be your best friend if there's no electricity! What if the city, county or national electrical grids are sabotaged and there is no power? What if your utilities get cutoff because you couldn't afford to pay? Therefore, if at all possible you should purchase a generator.

Also purchase staples like peanut butter and jelly, soup, crackers, beef stock and chicken stock. You can live off liquids! Buy canned meats like tuna fish, chicken, salmon and sausages. They key is to store items that have a long shelf life, that don't need to be cooked or can be cooked on a hot plate, BBQ grill, or small fire pit. You may also need a lighter or matches for the grill. Last, but certainly not least, one thing most people typically forget when stocking up is the very important item of toilet tissue.

Ladies should also remember to purchase feminine hygiene products in bulk. You just don't know what will be in short supply but high demand, so be prepared!

If you are a Christian openly professing Christ, food and other necessities may be in short supply for you! Intolerance and outright hatred of Christians will increase even more after the Rapture and necessities could be withheld from God's people. But do not be fearful because God will supply all your needs and He will take care of you! So if you realize that you missed the Rapture, get to the store quickly!

There will be widespread food shortages

There will be devastating hunger across the land and many will die from starvation. The Book of Revelation foretells that millions will die from famine, one-third of the sea life will be destroyed and one-third of the earth's water will be poisoned and unfit for human consumption.

Sooner or later, the food supply and the reserves will begin to diminish. Yes, they will. No matter what the media is allowed to report, it will be worse.

There will not be truthful or accurate media reports about the true state of affairs. They will be directed by the government (for public safety reasons) to withhold the actual truth so it will not induce widespread panic.

Make an effort to go outside your regular neighborhood and go to different grocery stores for your purchases. Shop at the warehouse stores and discounted grocers to purchase large quantities and stock up. Try to use cash! The reasons for using cash as much as possible will be discussed in the next chapter.

During these difficult times remember to pray and call on the Lord for help in times of trouble. Do not trust the news reports saying everything is alright and under control! Trust and rely on God.

Final thoughts… you will hear some Bible prophecy teachers say that these things will only happen in the nations where the Anti-Christ is ruling and will not happen in the United States. But who wants to take that chance? Millions in America will be gone in the Rapture. Many people remain optimistic about America during the Tribulation, hoping she will miss the wrath of God. Pray for God's mercy if you are living through the Tribulation Period because America will be judged for her sins and will go through the Great Tribulation.

Additional Reading and Reference:
Revelation Chapters 6, 8, and 9

Chapter 5

The List - Money
(Instructions)

Some of the things listed herein may or may not happen right away. When and if they do, you probably won't know about it until it's too late. So be prepared. Knowledge is power!

Money

- Get disciplined about your spending now!
- Use cash – eliminate or limit using credit cards
- Live beneath your means – stop living on credit
- Save some money and have access to it
- Long terms assets must have liquidity
- Get cash - keep cash on hand at all times
- Keep some cash safely hidden at home
- Keep small bills on hand ($1's, $5's, and $10's)
- No large bills, nothing over a $20 bill

In emergency situations "cash is king" when banks are closed and ATMs are down (these are lessons learned from the aftermath of Hurricane Katrina). When you get your paycheck, which for most people is typically direct deposit, cash it out after you pay the bills and keep some cash on hand.

If you get a paper check, cash it out. You should begin now to scale back spending and use cash as much as possible. We cannot imagine how harsh and difficult times will become. Since a lot people don't read much anymore and don't know anything about history, they won't know where things are headed and know that history does repeat itself!

America in Decline

Our founding documents are trampled upon and totally disregarded on a daily basis. Basic human and civil rights are being eroded and the governing bodies are out of control. Government agencies collect tons of data on law abiding citizens and even seize personal property. We've seen this happen before, world history reveals regimes and governments that tracked and monitored their citizens, and none was for the good of the people. Debit and credit card usage is tracked, tons of other personal and private data is collected, stored and even sold (to whom and for what purposes... who really knows).

How many scandals have surfaced within the last couple of years about major companies, banks and other financial institutions getting hacked and millions of credit card accounts, pin numbers, emails and passwords were stolen? This is just a precursor for the Anti-Christ tracking system.

In the last chapter, it was suggested you visit various neighborhood stores for grocery purchases and especially if you are buying large quantities. You and your spending habits cannot be tracked as easily when using cash! When it's within your control, remember to use cash as much as possible after the Rapture! This is important because as of right now, there remain too many unknowns about the true state of the U.S. economy and how close it is to the brink of the monetary system failing. The system is currently being stabilized by the Federal Reserve printing and pumping money into circulation to stave off inflation.

"These things are not meant to scare you, but to educate, prepare and protect you!"

Surely this is a lot to take in and to wrap your head around, but what was once a decent and normal lifestyle will no longer be the norm. The Rapture is a game-changing event for all of mankind. Paranoia, fear, control and deception will lead to many new changes and new laws not only in the U.S. but across the world!

In society and culture today, everything is monitored: emails, texts, phone calls. With cameras at every stoplight and every corner store tracking every move, is that really a good thing? Is it for safety, crime prevention, security or something else entirely different we don't know about? Can it be for the good of society or is it a sign of the new world order?

Boasters and Braggers Beware!

Be very careful what you share with others! After the Rapture, be careful not to share too many details of your personal survival plan to those outside of your immediate family or very close friends. Stop sharing financial matters with others and only share with the people whom you would trust with your life! Do not boast or brag about items you have stored for safekeeping like cash, food, weapons, medicine, etc.

When people are struggling to survive in hard times, trying to meet basic needs of food, water and shelter, they will do whatever it takes to endure those dire circumstances. Many witnessed this first hand during the aftermath of Hurricane Katrina when some awfully terrible things were done for survival.

Therefore be careful not to share too much of your personal information. No, this is not being paranoid, but using the wisdom of God. Some scripture references are:

Exodus 35:31 And he hath filled him with the spirit of God, in wisdom, in understanding, and in knowledge, and in all manner of workmanship.

Proverbs 3:5-6 Trust in the Lord with all thine heart; and lean not unto thine own understanding. In all thy ways acknowledge him, and he shall direct thy paths.

Proverbs 4:5-8 Get wisdom, get understanding: forget it not; neither decline from the words of my mouth. Forsake her not, and she shall preserve thee: love her, and she shall keep thee. Wisdom is the principal thing; therefore get wisdom: and with all thy getting get understanding.

Proverbs 8:12 I wisdom dwell with prudence and find out knowledge of witty inventions.

Isaiah 33:6 And wisdom and knowledge shall be the stability of thy times, and strength of salvation: the fear (reverence) of the Lord is his treasure.

James 1:5 If any of you lack wisdom, let him ask of God, that giveth to all men liberally, and upbraideth not; and it shall be given him.

To live on through the Tribulation and remain safe, you must operate in the wisdom of God and call on the help of the Holy Spirit so you will not be deceived by the media, all the propaganda and the newly created false religion. There will also be new technologies and ground breaking innovations that will "revolutionize" industries such as healthcare, intelligence and the military.

You must have the wisdom of God at the forefront of all you do. Praying and seeking God's wisdom in even the simplest of decisions and direction on what to do and what not to do will be critical to survival and not being deceived. Most of the world is asleep concerning the times in which we live. We are "living in the last days!" This means that the Church Age is soon to be over and the rapture is at hand. Jesus could come any day!

If you are reading this book *before* the Rapture you may never have to experience death and can be caught up to Heaven in the Rapture of the Church!

If you are a Christian, but are not where you should be in Him, make it right with God right now. Repent of your sins, forgive others and let go of past hurts, accept Jesus as savior and lord, and then move forward in Him.

"Read your Bible and Pray Every Day"
This will keep your heart and mind focused on God

Prepare your heart and make sure your salvation is eternally secure. If you do not have a church home, I pray you find a good bible believing church that teaches the whole counsel of God. Get plugged in and get busy for the Lord! This message needs to be heard... the message of love, hope and eternal redemption in Jesus Christ.

Chapter 6

The List - Spiritual
(Instructions)

The overall true message of Bible prophecy is God loves us, Satan is defeated and we win! But Satan has convinced most Christians the Book of Revelation is too deep and confusing like an unsolvable puzzle no one can understand, many have fallen into that trap and will never read it. Don't let that be you!

Spiritual

- If you don't have a Bible, get one or two immediately
- Get trustworthy and reputable Bible based books
- Get the Bible on CDs and DVDs (not downloads)
- Hide them for safekeeping
- Keep on hand an old DVD or CD player
- Get lots of batteries or battery charger
- Fellowship with other Christians you trust
- Pray every day

It is highly recommended to get an <u>actual</u> Bible book, even several Bibles of various translations. The real book is recommended versus an online site or an app because so many people have never been to church and wouldn't know if someone quoting scripture or poetry! So many people don't even know what's in the Bible. So to avoid deception and false preaching, get a Bible before...

The Bible will be "Outlawed"

After the Rapture, the Bible and other Christian material will be outlawed and considered contraband. You could find yourself in serious trouble for having them! Even now the Bible and many fundamentals of the faith are being eroded and erased from daily life.

The God-haters are becoming bolder and more outspoken in the hatred of all things good and especially all things pertaining to God. So gather up several Bibles and hide them for safe-keeping. Use wisdom when sharing them! Most people don't know much about history and don't recognize eliminating God from society, banning the Bible and books in general that history is repeating itself right now!

The foundation of modern day liberalism desires society to rid itself entirely of all notions relating to God, Christians and Christianity. They want to believe that God is dead or that He never really existed.

Some of what we see happening in churches, government and society today have the same underlying anti-God factors that have destroyed other nations. Historical evidence shows countries that were once open to Christianity, but became more enlightened and liberal in their belief systems, leading their countries into socialism and then communism. In your studies, research leaders like Stalin in Russia, Castro in Cuba, Hitler in Germany or Mao in China and you will find alarming similarities in these countries and the U.S. today; we're not that far from socialism (and socialism is not that far from communism).

"Socialism <u>tolerates</u> Christianity to certain extent, but Communism <u>eradicates</u> it from society"

Socialist and communist forms of government are generally atheist in their belief systems who ardently oppose the concept of capitalism and a free market driven economic society producing goods, etc... sound familiar?

It's unfortunate some ministers of the gospel have aligned themselves (albeit some unintentionally) with a secular progressive and politically correct agenda, which is diametrically opposed to the gospel of Jesus Christ.

Typically, secular progressives want nothing to do with God, Jesus or the Bible and want to eradicate the Bible completely out of society! They refuse acknowledge the existence of God and do not understand or see the need why anyone believes it or relies on the crutch of religion.

There has been research and surveys done that reveal a high percentage of evangelicals really don't know much about the Bible or don't read it at all. These types of Christians are easily swayed and misinformed. Many believers are spiritually inept, biblically illiterate and out of sync with God, His way of doing things and being right. The Bible remains relevant and is not outdated and will be anointed to change lives forever!

The Ten Commandments are still valid for today! God is still against sin. It's not because He doesn't want you to have any fun, but sin is of the devil, sin separates man from God and the wages of sin is death. Satan is the chief liar, thief and destroyer of all that is good.

John 10:10 The thief cometh not, but for to steal, and to kill, and to destroy: I am come that they might have life, and that they might have it more abundantly.

God does not "wink" at sin as being permissible just because we're living in the 21st century! It is vital you get into a good Bible teaching church that will not compromise the Word of God. It is for this reason that it's important to fellowship with other like minded Bible believers to stay strong in the Lord.

This gospel of Jesus Christ has been repackaged into New Age spirituality and has crept into a lot of churches and denominations. Many of the church plants in the late 1990's and early 2000's leading to the phenomenal mega church growth the last 15-20 years were the offspring of the New Age movement. No longer was the Holy Spirit, the Blood of Jesus, sin and repentance spoken of in church.

The true path to God and eternal life is not found by following the societal norms which are fleeting, nor the political correctness of the day which is ever changing. The Bible says to seek Christ with your whole heart, stay strong in the Lord and in the power of His might! Don't follow the crowd if the crowd is not right with God.

Matthew 7:13 "Enter ye in at the strait gate: for wide is the gate, and broad is the way, that leadeth to destruction, and many there be which go in thereat."

To be able to withstand the deception and persecution of living for God after the Rapture, do these things to remain strong in the Lord:

Read the Bible – Everyday

- Listen to it on your devices, phones and tablets. Just keep on reading, listening and viewing.
- Ask the Holy Spirit to help you understand what you are reading
- Seek the Holy Spirit's help and guidance for wisdom in everyday situations
- Practice the presence of God by singing worship songs, hymns and spiritual songs

Pray – Everyday

- Prayer is simply talking to God

- Pray about everything that touches your life

- When you pray don't do all the talking, get quiet and spend some time listening. Your inner man (spirit being) will hear the leading of the Lord

- Pray for your family and friends

- Pray for your safety and the safety of others

- Pray and confess the "blood of Jesus covers me and protects me in all situations"

- Pray in the Holy Ghost (praying in tongues)

Other Important Actions

- Take communion on a regular basis

- Play anointed worship music in your home/car

- Fellowship with other like-minded believers

- Stay mentally and physically strong

You can do all these things now, before the Rapture of the Church. I pray you stay strong in the Lord, be ready and be waiting and waiting for His return!

Chapter 7

The List - Protection
(Instructions)

Basic Protection

You will need to be able to protect yourself and your family. You must be prepared to do whatever it takes and whatever ways you deem prudent and necessary!

Just imagine how chaotic, riotous and crazy the days will be all around the world immediately following the Rapture. With many people no longer going to work, basic services will be in drastic decline. How many days will it take for cities to look and smell like a garbage heap? What about the food and water supply, is it safe? What about the national electrical grids, micro grids and interconnections? Will they be up and running could they be jeopardy of sabotage or attack? A large enough EMP (electro-magnetic pulse) attack could permanently destroy all electronics and technological defenses crippling the nation, sending it back to a world equivalent to the 1800s.

With all the utter chaos America's enemies may seize the opportunity to strike. Are there enough essential emergency personnel remaining that are willing to serve and protect? Will the national security and intelligence agencies be adequately staffed? There are so possible scenarios and unimaginable events that could happen. Fear and panic will be rampant and everything will be out of control and just crazy!

There are so many basic but essential services that most people never give a second thought to on any given day. We go the ATM and we get money. We go the grocery store and food is on the shelves. Then we go to the fast food place, order the super huge value meal... but all of this will change.

"The monetary system will collapse"

The monetary system as we know it today is being sustained by the Federal Reserve by printing and putting money in circulation to keep long term recession and inflation at bay. The dollar is barely worth the paper it is printed on and the U.S. is so far in debt it will NEVER get out! Being $17 trillion in debt, it is not a good thing that several anti-God and really anti-American countries hold our notes and carry our paper.

Remember, the government was never meant to take care of you... GOD is your source!

Proverbs 22:7 says: "The rich ruleth over the poor, and the borrower is servant to the lender." This is one of the main reasons why the U.S. is no longer a respected super-power in the world and is not a key player at the end of the ages. You have no real power when you are enslaved to debt.

People will feel hopeless and devastated by the loss of their loved ones and then on top of that the economy fails and disintegrates as well… if I were living in that kind of a new reality, I would be seriously thinking about how to protect myself and my family members. Turmoil and lawlessness will rule the day until martial law is declared.

Protection

- Secure items of self defense, ammo, etc.
- Pepper spray, a taser, a baseball bat, etc.
- An old-fashioned hand saw, ax, hammer
- A fully functional alarm system at your home
- Dead bolt locks on doors / window coverings
- Purchase OTC pain relievers, medicines, etc.
- Fully stocked First Aid Medical Kit
- Have a secure safe-room (if possible)

I am not advocating the legal purchase of a firearm, which of course is your constitutional right as a U.S. citizen as granted and protected under the Second Amendment… that would be "politically incorrect."

If per chance the Second Amendment is still intact during the Tribulation period, most would agree it's a basic human right is for a person to able to defend and protect him or herself. Do whatever it takes to physically protect yourself and your family against riotous looters, criminals and those who would harm you for food or water! You can also protect yourself (somewhat) with the some of the items listed like pepper spray or a baseball bat, etc.

Did You Know?

In the last quarter of 2012 the government began buying millions of rounds of all types of ammunition and also began to stockpile weapons? During this same time, politicians were seeking to introduce legislation to repeal the Second Amendment of the U.S. Constitution, which provides American citizens the right to bear arms (i.e., the right to legally purchase/own). These moves sought to make it illegal for citizens to have weapons in their home for protection or even for hunting. Isn't that interesting?

Many of our medical personnel, doctors, nurses, firefighters, police, paramedics and many others relied upon for emergency services will also be gone in the Rapture, leaving gaps in the numbers of those needed to help protect and serve in medical emergencies. Therefore, keep a fully stocked First Aid Kit with pain relievers, bandages, disinfectant and other necessary items.

With concerns for the old outdated electrical power grids in this country, outages could become commonplace. Keep a good old-fashioned hand saw, an ax and hammer on hand, because if the power is out... power tools won't work. You may need to cut firewood for heat or cooking, and those items could also be used for self-defense and protection.

Pray for Protection and Safety, but also have a <u>Plan</u> and <u>Prepare</u>!

If you've missed the Rapture, it would also be wise to have a charcoal BBQ grill (not propane), with charcoal briquettes and lighter fluid if needed. It may be needed for cooking meals on the grill in case there is no electricity, gas or heat. Firewood, newspapers and magazines will be needed for kindling to start a small fire, hence the reason for a lighter or matches.

After the Rapture with the Christians gone, environmental activists will have much more freedom to enforce some of their more radical agendas; so be careful chopping down a tree for firewood, it could be a crime with severe punishment or penalties!

Prayerfully consider the suggestions noted herein and then come up with your own plan for protection and safety. I know these suggestions and "The List" will not be popular or widely-held views.

I understand these are all things people don't even want to think about let alone prepare for! But after the Rapture, the days in which people will be living on the earth will be very different from today. The safety of your family, food, water and medical supply will be vitally important and could be a matter of life or death.

Online Protection

This book would not be complete without reviewing additional forms of protection that are also very important. The next chapter will look at online protection and security precautions.

What you do online whether it's email, web surfing, posting on various sites or even texting is known as a "digital footprint." Be aware and careful of what is posted onto social media, what you blog, "like" and share. There is tons of information already collected on every citizen and it now begins as early as birth, so know that...

"Monitoring will to increase, not decrease"

Chapter 8

Role of Technology in the Last Days
(Explanations)

Today's every increasing technology is central to end times Bible prophecy and technically ushering in the Tribulation period. These will be tremendous tools for the Anti-Christ system(s), all of which are already in place. Many technological discoveries align perfectly with end times Bible prophecy.

If the Rapture has not happened yet and based on what is transpiring in the economy and markets, in healthcare, education, government, political, religion, family and social issues, surely you recognize by now that we are living in the last days! It's time to call upon the wisdom of God for each and every decision we make. It's time to be prepared spiritually, time to be ready to meet Jesus, because time is short.

There are some mind blowing technologies that many people don't know or wouldn't even believe exist!

With rapidly expanding technology, scientists have been able to decode many of nature's secrets. One very interesting one is the newly created insect drones. Scientist and engineers have developed the first flying insect inspired drone can be used not only for surveillance, but also for nuclear capabilities! This micro-drone technology can be used for spying, militarized tactics or weaponry or even bioterrorism.

A major online retailer revealed development of their drone technology for delivery of small packages right to your doorstep via drone, all within a few hours of an actual online purchase!

So as you might imagine, the technology world is expanding at a phenomenal rate, faster than we know about since most of us don't have intelligence security clearance! The Bible said in the last days knowledge would increase. Technology is exploding so fast, the device you purchase today is outdated before you even get it home!

Daniel 12:4 But thou, O Daniel, shut up the words, and seal the book, even to the time of the end: many shall run to and fro, and knowledge shall be increased.

During the Great Tribulation, could there be times when major computer systems are shut down (on purpose) to gain or maintain control of the populace by withholding or limiting access to basic essential services like food, medicine or healthcare? Do you find that hard to believe?

Was there such an experiment in 3Q2013 with the turning off a major government computer system? Some think so. For example, government computers went down for several hours on a Saturday morning when thousands of people across 17 states were not able to use their food stamp debit cards to purchase groceries. The government's vendor said it was a system glitch with a small connectivity issue after a routine test of a backup.

Who does a backup or scheduled maintenance on a major system like that at 10 a.m. on a Saturday morning when most users are using the system?

Was it a Test Run?

There are some prophecy teachers and bloggers who believe this was a "test run" to gauge public reaction or outcry to monetary system failures (debit and credit system) and lack of access to food services being shut down for a few hours. The outcome was mass mayhem, disorder and even riots ensued! Was it really a system glitch or test of predicted outcomes?

Did you know that data has been (and is being) collected on most people living in the U.S.? Do you use the internet or a cell phone? Of course you do, therefore your data has probably been collected, copied, stored and sold. Oh, but you say that you never gave consent for that level of data mining or personal intrusion on your privacy?

Do you have a credit card, an email account or do you post to online sites? Ever download an app? When you download apps for those addictive games, videos, and any of those fun but essential apps, you provided "consent" to access your device and with that agree to allow each and every company access to the following:

- Emails accounts, contents and contacts
- Job, home, family and health history
- Bank accounts, financial records, credit cards
- GPS and other tracking services

When the company asked for permission to access your device, you quickly clicked OK or Accept. Data has been collected from your phone calls and texts, emails and social sites; information is also collected on where you bank, shop and eat! This information is collected by government agencies that oftentimes don't even need a court order and is often sold for a profit to various other companies.

All of this information can be stored in a small but very powerful *nano chip,* which is smaller than a grain of rice and can be inserted anywhere and on anything!

This chip is in every phone, tablet, laptop and desktop, but can also be inserted under fingertips, in the palm of the hand and even in eye contact lenses!

Some of these technologies are not new (in technological terms) as veterinarians have tested and used the "nano-pet" technology as a cloud based pet recovery database system for years!

This user acceptance was expanded to the toy industry (for early adoption); kids inserted trackers into their little teddy bears in case it got lost. They have since grown up at ease with trackers, GPS and other locater apps openly embracing tracking. Eventually, taking the mark of the Anti-Christ (which is 666) will be no big deal. Hey, it's just another tattoo used for identity and security. Invisible ink (also used in tattoos) has been tested, patented and is in use today. People might not even know they've been inked.

Revelation 13:15-18 tells us that during the Great Tribulation that no man will be able to buy or sell without the "mark" which is 666. Some prophecy teachers say the mark will not be in America, but the radio frequency identification (RFID) tracking chip is marketed as a "child safety" and will be required for all children starting at birth in just a few years.

Throughout history, we have seen that man has not done well with so much power at his disposal. Power corrupts and these technology systems will be powerful tools in the hands of the Anti-Christ. Just think, if he wants to rid the world of the remaining Christians, he has all that information at his disposal.

So just a word of caution: be wise and attentive to any mandates for _unilateral adherence_ to _any one system_.

When you read the scriptures, ask the Holy Spirit to open the eyes of your understanding on things being described here. While no one can know exactly what will happen or how bad times will be after the Rapture; it is safe to say that it will be worse than anyone could have ever imagined.

Are you an "early adopter?"

An early adopter embraces new technology before the general population. These tech junkies love all the latest and greatest devices and rush to get these new gadgets and gizmos before they are available to the public. These techno geeks even volunteer to serve as testers for major companies and yes some are on the payroll. Many new technologies are being tested by early adopters, and others are tested by private companies, the military and governmental agencies.

Remember when everything went digital and high definition? Did you wonder why it was mandated that all televisions transitioned? Everyone had to get a dish, digital cable or a converter box to even receive a signal. What was the _real reason_ for these swooping industry changes? It could be as simple as innovation or more money, or it could be more profound than the obvious.

Is Your TV Smarter than You?

All types of electronics such as cars, phones, tablets, laptops, gaming systems, cable boxes and many more have global positioning systems, cameras and microphones, which are remotely programmable. Since these products can be turned on anytime from anywhere, what you say and do in the privacy of your home, bedroom or office is no longer private if there's a tablet, TV or phone nearby.

These devices have the capability to also be remotely monitored. Bet you didn't know that! This may sound funny, but in the very near future you will need to watch what you say and do in the privacy of your own home! Game consoles and cable boxes can be "turned on" and you could be monitored... without your knowledge! I did not say without your consent, remember you provided consent when the item was purchased or you signed up for services. [Always Read the Fine Print!]

Naiveté is NOT a Virtue!

You may have missed it, but the world yawned at the news of a groundbreaking software patent by a major U.S. company that actually monitors you while watching TV! This software can be found in digital cable boxes, DVR's, gaming systems, and can be programmed (meaning can be turned on) to survey the room to determine not only what you are watching and here's the scary part... actually listen to what you are saying and doing in the room!

"Big Brother is definitely watching and only God knows who else!"

This ambient user software can monitor how many people are in the room, what is being said and even what you are doing. It can send relevant personalized commercial ads to your TV or tablet. The software can listen or scan conversations in the room or conversations on your phone. It then picks up "key words" that send signals to the system and it then sends specific commercials to play on **your** television, based on what you've been talking about!

Surely this is great technology for intelligence and military usage, maybe not so great for consumers. For example: if you're talking about buying a new truck, the software picks up on key words and then can fine-tune truck commercials to your television!

This software can also be configured with infrared sensors to determine the types of objects in the room, like lamps, furniture, picture frames and will even be able to determine what type of pet is in the home. No longer will you need to guess about possible dog food choices. This system will send specific and targeted commercials with ads for Fido's food directly to you!

The possibilities of what types of information that can be, will be or has already been gathered about our no longer private lives are endless!

Experts will say these types of technology are most likely several years away, even if the patents are eventually granted. But the ambient actions of users' technology has been tested in the consumer arena as far back as 2008. After the Rapture, these technologies can be used for adverse intentions, so buyer-beware!

**"These things are not meant to scare you,
but to inform and educate you"**

This information is not meant to scare you to hide out in the basement or head to the backwoods to become a doomsday prepper, but to inform and educate you! Living in the last days, it is the preparation of the heart that is of vital importance.

There is still time to make things right with God! Have you accepted Jesus? He paid the ultimate price for your sin on the cross at Calvary. If you haven't done so already, ask Jesus to come into your heart right now. There is still time to secure your eternal salvation with the Lord!

The days on the earth after the Rapture will be like nothing anyone could have ever imagined. The Bible says (II Timothy 3:1-5) in the last days that difficult and perilous (dangerous, unsafe, risky) times will come.

So today as you read this *before* the Rapture of the Church, know that everything is in place and nothing else needs to happen before Jesus comes.

You have been asleep at the wheel if you cannot see how society and culture is becoming increasingly anti-God and intolerant of anything and everything Christian. This along with the rapid increase of technology, the condition of the apostate (worldly/secular) Church and especially with what is going on with Israel... you should look up, because Jesus is coming soon!

Chapter 9

Where Was the Church?
(Explanations)

Jesus Christ is coming back for a glorious church, one that is praying and watching for His return. Jesus is not coming for a lukewarm, barely saved, worldly, so-called Christians living their lives however they please and not in accordance with His Word. If you were Jesus... would you?

The Church is living in the most difficult times in modern history. Sharing your testimony for Jesus has almost been relegated as hate speech. Christians around the world are being killed for their beliefs in Jesus Christ. Yet many Christians in America are hiding in the closet, afraid and ashamed to outwardly live for and proclaim Jesus.

Many will ask "where was the Church *before* all this happened?" How come they didn't tell me?

Many will want to know why they never heard about living in the last days, end time events, Bible prophecy, the book of Revelation and that Jesus was coming soon. This message must be shared and taught at church, at home, on the phone, where ever you meet and hang out with people!

Living in these last days, many ministers yielded to ministry and societal peer pressure and cultural norms preaching secular progressive watered down sermons, following the fads, trends or the political correctness of the day. Some preachers even agreed that the scriptures are outdated and in need of updating to fit modern times. That spirit does not come from Heaven! It was rare to hear a sermon on living free from sin, or the blood of Jesus or being filled with the Holy Spirit. Sermons were based on feel good motivational messages and often bypassed the Holy Bible.

The Church...
"got caught up in the world and lost influence"

For some in the Church, being acceptable "IN" the world has become the new wave of Christianity. Christians have snuggled up so close with the world you cannot tell the difference between saint and sinner. A commonly held belief is one must look like the world and act like the world to win the world. But does that really line up with the word of God?

It also became increasingly rare to find an actual Bible in the Church. Since the songs and scriptures are projected on the large screens, attendees don't see the need to bring their Bible. In some churches the scriptures aren't even read anymore! Don't get me wrong, this is not being judgmental but stating the facts in explaining how the church lost some of its influence in the last days.

The Church...
"got into competition with itself"

The church world embraced "mega mania" by focusing too heavily on adding gyms, coffee shops, food courts, fitness centers and movie theatres to reach the un-churched. The church world was known more for its choir, concerts, parties, programs and other worthwhile activities, instead of and often at the expense of solid Bible preaching, teaching and discipleship, outreach and missions. Yet this became the new church growth model!

God is certainly into to church growth and wants His house full. Programs, choirs and all the other new necessities the church must have are good and needed. Yes, numbers and church growth are important, but it should not be an "either/or" situation. The word of God should never be removed, watered down or compromised to get people to come to church! It is possible to have both and to do both successfully! The Word must be first, foremost and have final authority in the church!

Many congregations struggled to keep their doors open and found themselves outdated against the online internet churches and other churches in their communities that have strobe lighting, flashing laser light shows with rock band entertainment style worship, coffee and bagel bars, exercise classes and other programs larger churches offered. God's churches should never be in competition with each other, but united in support of one another to be a greater blessing in the community.

Women's ministry meetings became like red carpet celebrity type events so large and exclusive that other churches could not keep up or compete with a mere Bible study, prayer group, luncheon or a tea! If your church had women's ministry, it had to be event-driven because no one comes out just for intercessory prayer meeting!

Some preacher's egos grew out of control as their congregations grew. They got into boasting and bragging (under the guise of testifying about the goodness of God) how many people they had or how many services they were running, thus insinuating smaller congregations were out of the will of God! This brought about enmity amongst preachers and unspoken but fierce (ungodly) competition to keep up with the other Bishops, Apostles and Prophets.

Others in ministry had a false balance with too much emphasis concentrated on "building their ministry" with bigger buildings, television and secular businesses instead of the member's spiritual growth, discipleship, or missions, etc., and as a result the family and communities suffered.

The Church...
"became lethargic, apathetic and lazy"

Christians should attend church and get plugged into a local body of believers. Hebrews 10:25 instructs believers not to forsake the assembling of ourselves with other believers. Online resources, internet churches and teaching ministries should be a supplement to learning and growth. Sheep need to have a shepherd (pastor) to watch over their soul, to counsel and fellowship with on a personal level. Television ministries and online churches cannot look after, attend to, care for, console and comfort you as a good shepherd should. There is no accountability in sitting in front of a computer or phone. We must have the fellowship of other believers to stay strong in the Lord.

Lots of people just "check the box" to fulfill their religious obligation or to make themselves feel good for having attended Sunday services. For many, going to church was just another weekend obligation like getting a haircut or manicure, cutting the grass, going to the grocery store, the dry cleaners or shopping mall. People want and need to feel like they are part of a community so they go to church for socialization, or to network for business, even to find a date, but not really to seek and worship the Lord.

Lots of people consider themselves spiritual or religious, but have no relationship with God. They acknowledge the existence of the big man upstairs, but are not born-again. They want God but not Jesus, Christianity without Christ and don't believe in going to church. This is unscriptural and they are deceived! They blame their non-church attendance on too many hypocrites in the church, or too many sex and money scandals of church leaders.

The Church...
"lost its way in being religious"

But for every bad example of a fallen leader, there are thousands more examples of honorable, faithful and men and women full of integrity doing with work of the ministry and teaching the full counsel of the God's Word! There are some great churches and awesome pastors truly called by God and doing the work of the ministry! Not everyone followed the deceptive fads of the world.

These were just some, but certainly not all, examples of how the lukewarm Church lost some of its influence in the last days. But God is still holy and his Word never changes and remains vital for today.

Chapter 10

Revelation and Signs of the Second Coming of Christ
(Explanations)

Did you know that what most people would call "the end of the world" is not a biblically correct statement? It would be better stated to say at the "end of times" or now at the "end of the age" as we know it or better yet just the end of the Church Age.

The Rapture of the Church should not be confused with the Second Coming of Christ.

The Rapture event is **not** the Second Coming of Christ. That is yet to happen!

The Second Coming of Christ happens at the end of the Great Tribulation and ushers in the new millennium. Some key differences between the Rapture of the Church and the Second Coming of Christ are:

Rapture – believers meet Christ in the air
Second Coming – Christ returns to the Mount of Olives in Jerusalem to govern on the earth

Rapture – believers receive glorified immortal bodies
Second Coming – believers remain in natural body

Rapture – believers go to Heaven for seven years
Second Coming – all those in Heaven come back to earth; Satan is defeated and sealed up in the pit of Hell, the saints' rule and reign with Jesus

Rapture – deliverance of Church from wrath to come
Second Coming – delivers believers on earth who endured the wrath of the Great Tribulation

Rapture – only the saved, born-again true Church
Second Coming – deals with both the saved (eternal salvation) and the unrepentant (judgment)

Rapture – Satan remains free on earth to rule and openly deceive and is mainly uncontested
Second Coming – Satan is bound and thrown into the Abyss (Hell) for a thousand years

In which group do you want to accept Jesus? *Before* the rapture of the church or *After* the rapture of the church?

Hopefully you desire to go to Heaven at the Rapture versus trying to live through the Tribulation period! The Second Coming of Christ will take place at the end of the Great Tribulation as foretold in Revelation 19:1-16.

**If it's hard to go to church now,
it will be even more difficult after the Rapture!**

The book of Daniel describes this time as "one seven" year block consisting of two "times, time and half a time." This can be understood as 2yrs=times, 1yr=time and ½yr=half a time. This also equates to two 1,260 days or two 42-month periods. The first half of this time is called the Tribulation and the second half of this time is called the Great Tribulation.

References: Daniel 9:27; Revelation 12:14, 11:2-3, 13:5

The Book of Revelation reveals in great detail what transpires on the earth during the Tribulation. Either just right before or immediately following the Rapture is when the new world order leader (the Anti-Christ) comes on the scene to calm fears and tries to restore peace to a chaotic and distressed world after the Rapture of the Church and the attack on Israel.

The Bible foretells of a coalition of nations that will launch a surprise attack against Israel. These nations are modern day Russia and its Muslim allies.

Strategic intelligence, military and financial alliances between these anti-Israel nations are already forming! They will mount a large scale military attack against Israel, a small sovereign nation with great military strength. The surprise attack will utterly fail! This war is referred to as Ezekiel's war, when Israel is supernaturally protected by God and her enemies are destroyed and defeated (Ezekiel Chapters 38-39).

"There will be peace in the Middle East!"

The Anti-Christ steps onto the world scene, mostly likely from the podium of the United Nations and announces that he's brokered a seven year peace treaty with Israel. With this incredible achievement the Anti-Christ rises to the forefront with instant credibility and establishes himself as the new world leader. Here are some characteristics of the man of sin are:

- A Diplomatic Politician
- Handsome and Charming
- Well versed in the Rule of Law & Economics
- Charismatic Leader people will follow
- Strong Personality, Powerful, Arrogant
- Great Orator, Eloquent in Speech
- Strategic and Visionary
- Wicked, Evil, Liar and Demonic
- No desire for women

He is viewed as a great leader, a powerful man of peace and goodwill, but it is false! The Book of Daniel describes him as deceitful and a persecutor of the brethren (Daniel 7:21-25, 8:25). The world will love this man as he will calm fears after the Rapture and bring peace to the Middle East. He will say, do and perform many great works to win the hearts of man but his motives are ungodly and he is possessed by Satan himself.

Right at the halfway point of the Tribulation Period, he will break the peace treaty with Israel and show the whole world who he really is and what his satanic intentions are!

Who Is the Anti-Christ?

I believe too many people waste too much time trying to figure out who is the Anti-Christ and not enough time sharing the good news of the gospel of Jesus Christ to get people saved before the Rapture!

Over the years many world leaders have been identified as possible Anti-Christ candidates, but all have been wrong. The Bible does not provide insight to that information, so don't waste your time. Besides, if you are born-again and ready to meet Jesus, who cares about the identity of the Anti-Christ! You won't be here when he rises to power. Since the Bible only provides characteristics of the man of sin, there is no need for speculation.

The Bible does say the Anti-Christ is released <u>after</u> the Church has been caught up to Heaven and Jesus opens the first of seven seals (Revelation 6:1-2). However, given the times in which we live, it would be safe to say the man of sin is alive and of adult age living on the earth today.

> <u>II Thessalonians 2:3-4, 9</u> Let no man deceive you by any means: for that day shall not come, except there come a falling away first, and that man of sin be revealed, the son of perdition; Who opposeth and exalteth himself above all that is called God, or that is worshipped; so that he as God sitteth in the temple of God, shewing himself that he is God. Even him, whose coming is after the working of Satan with all power and signs and lying wonders.

The Jewish Temple is Rebuilt!

The Anti-Christ appears to be a friend of Israel after the peace treaty is signed and even allows them to rebuild their Temple. Upon completion, the Anti-Christ goes to the Temple and declares that he is the Messiah and God. A remnant of the Jewish people utterly rejects this blasphemy and flees for safety to the hills of Petra. They flee in fear of what appears to have the makings of another holocaust and they are right! The Anti-Christ will try to annihilate the Jewish people. He also sends the False Prophet to Rome to oversee the new religion designed solely to worship the Anti-Christ (and kill all those who don't worship him).

This new false religion mostly likely will setup headquarters in the Vatican City, which will no longer be under the rule of what was formerly known as the Roman Catholic Church. Many religious leaders at the Vatican (who were truly born-again) also went to Heaven in the Rapture as well as many, many other born-again Catholics.

The Anti-Christ will try to outlaw and ban all remaining denominations aligned with the Jehovah God. He will commission the False Prophet to further his satanic agenda by decree (or executive order) that all nations where the Anti-Christ reigns and rules must worship him as the new one and only "God."

Additional Signs of the Lord's Return

Chapter 12 of the Book of Daniel provides additional details as to the timing of the Lord's return. These are commonly called "signs of the times" in Bible prophecy. At the end of time, travel and knowledge will be greatly increased. Just within in the last 50 years or so, there has been tremendous advances travel.

This is not only in ground transportation (car, bus and train) but especially the advances in air and space travel. It seems like man just landed on the moon and now the space shuttle program has been outsourced to private companies! But one of the greatest Bible prophecies that have already come to pass is: the re-establishment of the nation of Israel.

It was prophesied in the Old Testament, in the books of Isaiah 66:7-8 and Ezekiel 37:21-22 that Israel's children would be brought home and they would be a nation.

Israel became a nation
May 14, 1948

This had to happen because of God's everlasting covenant with Abraham! If you've heard of replacement theology, know that it is false! The Church did not "*replace*" Israel as God's elect. In Genesis 12:3, God's covenant with Abraham was an *everlasting* covenant. In Romans 11:1-2, Paul answers the question if God cast away His people and the answer: God forbid! God has not cast away Israel.

There are other Bible prophecies that could not have been understood until modern days with all the technological advances. For example, Revelation 11:9 says the whole world will look upon two dead bodies lying in the streets of Jerusalem. How could our ancestors or even our grandparents think that could be possible?

Probably the greatest Bible prophecy of the Old Testament was that the Messiah was coming. Jesus Christ is the ultimate Bible prophecy fulfilled, in His virgin birth, His death, burial and resurrection!

With so many Bible prophecies already fulfilled, we can know with a certainty that prophecy in Revelation yet to unfold will come to pass.

God has promised that one day soon His Son Jesus will appear in the Heavens, with the shout of an archangel and the blowing of the trumpet, believers will meet Him in the sky, never experiencing death. Glory to God!

It's exciting to study end times prophecy and signs, Jewish history and other historical facts, current global events and even technology developments that were foretold (prophesied) in the Bible and are actually taking place today and will continue to do so into the near future.

Bible Prophecy Is Exciting!

The re-establishment of the nation of Israel is an incredible example of end time prophecy coming to pass right before our eyes. There are also signs in nature. The Bible says there will be an increase in earthquakes and signs in the Heavens like comets, blood moons and unusual weather patterns. It also says Bible prophecy will be understood more in the end times (Daniel 12:4).

I know this is a lot to comprehend, but the fact remains that God's word is exact and true. Whatever it says will come to pass, will come to pass. Believe it!

I've provided these explanations because if you remain on the earth *after* the Rapture, you must have a good working knowledge of the Bible to avoid being deceived by what's going on right before your very eyes! People trying to explain away what has really happened, saying it was not the Rapture at all.

There will be preachers and many others left behind who will repent and get right with God. Yet sadly there will be countless scores of others who will not repent. Their disdain and hatred towards God will grow deeper and they will fall into greater depravity and deception; the God haters will have great freedom.

If there are people you really care about, will you share this knowledge with them? Time is short.

As we all have said in the past: "I wouldn't wish that on my worst enemy." I pray this will be true and you won't let anyone you love and care about miss the Rapture and go through the Tribulation!

I pray you share Jesus and share these truths with them!

Chapter 11

The Great Tribulation
(Explanations)

The information contained herein would not be complete without providing an overview of what transpires during the Tribulation. For your own personal study this can be found in the Book of Revelation, Chapters 6 thru 19. These chapters detail the opening of the seals in Heaven which release the wrath and judgment of God, which are war, famine, and other horrible plagues that will happen during this 7-year period.

After the Rapture,
the Church Age is over

The Church Age was the designated time for Gentiles (all other non-Jewish people) to know and accept Jesus Christ. Remember, the Tribulation Period is not meant for Christians!

This 7-year slice of time has been set aside for God to provide a final opportunity before eternity for Israel to receive Jesus as Messiah, to deal with unrepentant sinners who still reject Jesus Christ, to defeat Satan and usher in the Kingdom Age which is the Millennial Reign of Jesus Christ on the earth.

The Book of Revelation chapters are not written in exact chronological order. It transitions between Heaven and earth, describing what is going on in Heaven with the saints and simultaneously what is happening on the earth during the Tribulation.

Revelation does describe in great detail the wrath of God upon earth and upon those who continue to rebel against Him. The following is an outline overview of what transpires during the Tribulation Period:

The Seven Seals are opened
(following the Rapture):

1. *Anti-Christ (false peace)
2. *War
3. *Famine
4. *Death
5. Martyrdom
6. Anarchy
7. Silence

Note: * denotes the Four Horsemen of the Apocalypse

The Seven Trumpets are judgments

(Tribulation Period is the first 3 ½ years):

1. 1/3 of the trees destroyed
2. 1/3 sea life destroyed
3. 1/3 water poisoned
4. 1/3 light is darkened
5. 1st Woe: demonic locusts released from Hell
6. 2nd Woe: fire & brimstone rains from Heaven
7. Christ's reign foreseen

The Seven Bowl (Vials) are judgments

(Great Tribulation is the last 3 ½ years):

1. Boils
2. All sea life destroyed
3. All water poisoned
4. Lethal, scorching sun
5. Deep darkness
6. Euphrates River dried up
7. Bowling ball size hail (100+ lbs)

Common misconceptions about the Tribulation and the Great Tribulation is that people think the first 3½ years will be a time of peace, partly due to the peace treaty in the Middle East. This is not true! Jesus opens the seals and it releases not only the Anti-Christ, but also war, death and famine! I don't see any peace anywhere in those judgments and this is a time of God's judgment and wrath.

The Anti-Christ comes to power with diplomacy and peace, but that is quickly abated as he rules with brute force, murder, war (and even nuclear war) to annihilate those who oppose him.

The Jewish people will be living under a sense of security and overall well being (due to the peace treaty) while rebuilding their Temple.

However, other nations of the world will be at war against the Anti-Christ which will be utterly devastating. Approximately one-fourth of humanity will die in the initial war during the Tribulation Period's first 3½ years and with today's population even after the Rapture, that still amounts to "millions" of people being killed.

The 2 Witnesses

During the Great Tribulation there will be tremendous famine, wars, nuclear war and massive death. Even after the 144,000 have finished preaching the gospel for the first 3½ years with multitudes receiving Jesus Christ (Revelation 7:9-17), God then sends two witnesses from Heaven to continue the work, preaching repentance and salvation through Jesus Christ. Many prophecy teachers differ on their opinions as to who these men are, but most believe the witnesses are Elijah and Enoch, while some believe they are Elijah and Moses. One Bible clue says "it is appointed unto to men once to die" (Hebrews 9:27).

The Anti-Christ will try to stop the Heavenly witnesses from preaching the gospel on the streets in Jerusalem. However, he is not successful! The witnesses must fulfill their mission to preach the last 3½ years during the Great Tribulation.

People can still receive Jesus and get saved during the time of the Great Tribulation, but they will "not be raptured" or go to Heaven. They remain on the earth and endure the torment of the Tribulation until the end. Some will be martyred for their faith. The 144,000 Jewish evangelists and all the Jewish and Gentiles who accepted Jesus will be caught up to Heaven at mid-Tribulation.

Near the very end of the Great Tribulation the witnesses will be shot and killed. The Anti-Christ will make a mockery of them by leaving their dead bodies on the streets in Jerusalem for three days, which is also Bible prophecy fulfilled (Revelation 11:3-13). The two witnesses are raised from the dead after three days and are also caught up to Heaven.

Those who worship the Anti-Christ and have taken the mark are so happy the witnesses are dead and no longer preaching that vile hate speech (which is the gospel of Jesus Christ), that they rejoice in the streets and celebrate by giving gifts to one another! They mistakenly think that now unrestrained sin, lasciviousness and evil finally have free reign on the earth.

But God is not done! After three days the entire world (live via satellite) sees the absolutely amazing event that happens next, their bodies raised from the dead and ascend into Heaven! Revelation 11:13 says the ground will shake with a massive earthquake when the witnesses are raised from the dead and that 7,000 people die from this resurrection earthquake. Shortly after this the Great Tribulation ends.

The Second Coming of Christ

This time Jesus Christ is coming back to earth with the Heavenly host and all the saints with Him. This is the Second Coming of Christ. Revelation 19:11-16 reads: "And I saw Heaven opened, and behold a white horse; and he that sat upon him was called Faithful and True, and in righteousness he doth judge and make war."

After destroying the 200-million man army in an instant at the Battle of Armageddon, the Anti-Christ and the False Prophet are thrown alive into the lake of fire (Revelation 19:20) and Satan is chained, bound and thrown into the abyss (Revelation 20:2). The Millennial Reign of Jesus Christ begins with... Peace on Earth.

Chapter 12

Final Thoughts...

My prayer is that this book has been a blessing to you and has been enlightening on matters concerning end times Bible prophecy. I don't want anyone to be caught unaware of what's yet to transpire living in the last days of the Church Age.

I hope you have a greater understanding about the Rapture of the Church and how it is differs from the Second Coming of Christ; and that you are now open and willing to actually study and read the Book of Revelation!

There are so many people in the world that don't know anything about God or His Word. Even in the body of Christ, so many people have never heard anything taught about prophecy or have never even opened their Bible to the Book of Revelation. They have no clue that we are living in the last days.

My goal was to make this book an easy and exciting read so people on any level can understand this message of hope, redemption and eternal life in Christ.

If you have missed the Rapture of the Church, this book will help guide you, spiritually, mentally and physically through the difficult days ahead and provide insight into what happens next.

If the Rapture has not happened yet, this book should serve as a warning and a witnessing tool. It will help you explain to family and friends about Jesus, the time in which we live, and that nothing else in prophecy needs to happen before the Rapture and that Jesus is coming soon!

And for those that believe Christians will be on the earth to actually go through the Tribulation, it is God's will you be *saved from* the wrath to come:

Romans 5:9
"Much more then, being now justified by his blood, we shall be saved from wrath through him."

1 Thessalonians 1:10
"And to wait for his Son from Heaven, whom he raised from the dead, even Jesus, which delivered us from the wrath to come."

1 Thessalonians 5:9
"For God hath not appointed us to wrath, but to obtain salvation by our Lord Jesus Christ"

It is Satan... that doesn't want you to read and understand the Holy Bible.

It is Satan... that doesn't want you to know how much God loves you and that Jesus Christ paid the price for your sin by providing for eternal life.

It is Satan... that doesn't want you to know and understand Bible prophecy because it clearly reveals his ultimate demise and defeat!

The message of Bible prophecy is God loves us, we-win and Satan is defeated! For too long now, Satan has convinced most people that the Book of Revelation is too deep and confusing, that it is like an unsolvable puzzle no one can ever fully understand. It's sad and unfortunate most Christians have never read it or will ever read it. Please don't let that be you!

Don't fall into silly arguments about why would a loving God send a person to Hell. That's just foolish talk. God doesn't send anyone to Hell. God made man with a free will to choose. So I ask why would anyone refuse the free gift of salvation and eternal life from a loving God who sent his Son to die for their sins?

The judgment and wrath of God will come. Heaven is real and Hell is real. God didn't make Hell for man; it was made for the rebellious fallen angel Lucifer (also called Satan) and his fallen angel cohorts. Satan hates you because of God and even more because of Jesus! Satan's plan is single fold: to kill, steal and destroy (John 10:10).

He hates God and since you were made in God's image, Satan hates you! His plan of action is to take as many as possible of God's people to Hell with him (forever). He knows his eternal fate and damnation, but do you know your divine destiny or eternal destination?

For those who still may not believe, let me ask you just what IF, for the sake of argument, what IF the Bible is true and you never believe on Jesus Christ?

You have all of <u>Hell</u> to gain and all of <u>Heaven</u> to lose!

My heartfelt prayer is that you will not slip over into eternity thinking there was more time to make it right with God now because tomorrow is not promised to anyone!

- ✓ If you're not saved, accept Jesus today
- ✓ For those already saved, stay saved!
- ✓ Live for Jesus, a holy life acceptable unto Him
- ✓ Tell others about Jesus before it's too late

Share the knowledge you've gained from this book! Time is running out to talk with loved ones and get them born-again. There is nothing else needs to happen in Bible prophecy before Jesus comes!

Get serious about the things of God and stop wasting time. Jesus is coming soon and *this thing is for real!*

Remember also to:

- ✓ Read the Bible everyday
- ✓ Get in a Bible believing church
- ✓ Go to church - there is strength in fellowship
- ✓ Pray and ask God for wisdom and direction
- ✓ Learn how to pray effectively and then pray!
- ✓ Receive the Baptism of the Holy Spirit

Settle this speaking in tongues thing once and for all; it is not of the devil! It is your personal prayer language spoken between you and God. Satan cannot defeat a believer who prays in the Holy Ghost! I did not say there wouldn't be any challenges, but God will deliver you out of them all. You cannot be defeated if you do not quit!

Last but certainly not least, if the Rapture has already happened when you are reading this, I pray you remain safe, live for Jesus as best you can, follow the instructions from "The List" and above all else...

"Do Not Take the Mark of the Beast!"

This mark could be any form of a universal number or barcode containing all your personal data (i.e., emails, bank accounts, credit cards, financial history, driver's license, passport, medical history). The mark is a major component of the Anti-Christ tracking system so do **not** take this mark!

If you have not accepted Jesus Christ as your savior and lord, don't delay, do it today! I know this sounds like a broken record, saying that you must be born-again over and over and over again, but it's just that important, it's of eternal importance.

**"There is nothing more important in life
than making a decision for Christ."**

It is what you've done with Jesus Christ, either accepting Him or rejecting Him that will determine your salvation and eternal destination; not your good works, good looks, or living a good life, so seek the Lord now while He can be found. God bless you.

And behold, I come quickly
Revelation 22:7

Hope to see you in Heaven & Eternity!

Joan Lightsey

About the Author

Joan "Pastor Joanie" Lightsey is an ordained minister of the gospel serves alongside her husband Dr. Ernest B. Lightsey, the Founder and Senior Pastor at the church they pioneered, Word of Faith Fellowship Church in Overland Park, Kansas.

Pastor Joanie is an anointed bible teacher who serves as Assistant Pastor and Executive Administrator of Word of Faith Fellowship Church and Caring Within Ministries which includes the Caring Within Our Community Food Pantry.

She founded the WOFFC Bible Prophecy School and hosts Bible prophecy seminars, conferences and a weekly radio broadcast on "Living in the Last Days."

She also leads the Women of the Word Ministry, the Covenant Girls Bible Club and Next Level Living: Christian Life Coaching and Mentoring to Women.

A wife, mother and grandmother, Pastor Joanie has been successful in business with entrepreneurial endeavors and a corporate career spanning three decades.

Her heart's desire is to teach believers who they are in Christ and how to walk in victory in every area of life.

Made in the USA
San Bernardino, CA
08 March 2014